## A Message from Mani

We have all experienced times and situations that have left us
feeling broken, confused, and ready to give up. As we
encounter life's difficulties, our focus should be on what we
"grow through" and not what we "go through." Growth is often
uncomfortable, but always necessary! It is so easy to listen to
the voices in our heads, illuminating every negative
connotation based on society's standards and our own
misfortune. But I declare that it is high time that we take back
our Power and begin to grow from those things that once made
us weak! My mission is to encourage you to allow yourself the
grace to grow. I have heard that it takes 21 days to break a
habit, or to form a new one. Grace may be defined as an
extended period of special favor, and it allows us the audacity
to get up and begin again when we fall. With growth, you will
discover the hidden you, and you will learn to fall madly in
love with the masterpiece that you are. It is my sincerest prayer
that at the end of this journey together, you will be inspired to
Smile again, Hope again, and live every day in your authentic
Truth!

# My Story!

Today was a beautiful day! I cried for twenty minutes as I awakened from my safe place. The place where there's no worries, no fears, and no shame. The place where I am beautiful, and they love me! I tried to close my eyes again, I was not ready to get up and face the sad reality of the mess of a life that I had made. But I was fully awake now, and reconvening safety was not an option. I had no choice but to get up. I got up, drowned my tears in water, and put my pants on, one leg at a time. I had work and school and children, so no time to sit and sob for long. You see, I grew up with the notion that I was not as beautiful or gifted as the others. So, I was never really worth-it! I felt I had to work extra hard to get what the "pretty girls" got with ease. I had gotten so used to being disregarded that I began to isolate myself from possible beneficial social gatherings. When I was forced to engage, I tried to lead with laughter. I thought that if I could make them laugh, I could make them like me. It was actually quite sad though, I walked around with a happy mask while inside feeling like a walking trauma story. I had been so used and abused in relationships that maltreatment was expected. By the age of twenty-six, I had four children with three different men and people made sure I felt disgusting about it. I didn't count my two babies that passed early in life. My first child, Nia, was stillborn when I was just fourteen years old. After her demise, I went back to school pretending as if she were still in the land of the living. For some strange reason, I was ashamed to let my peers know that she had passed away. School was another place where I could never fit in. I felt as if the students did not like me, and neither did the teachers. In fact, during my junior year of high school, I had an English teacher who told me that "I would never be good for anything but lying on my back!" Boy did Ms. Whitehead, my eleventh-grade English teacher, serve me a hard pill to swallow. I wish she knew that those words created trauma that followed me into my adulthood. At the tender of age twenty-four, I found out that I was pregnant again. This pregnancy was so rough, that I even considered abortion at one point. The relationship with the baby's father was both abusive and toxic, but it's as if I were addicted to the pain. Although abortion was a strong possibility, my heart would not allow me to destroy the life that was growing inside me. I delivered my sweet baby, Ayanna, prematurely and I fell in love with her instantly. She spent her first few weeks of life in the NICU, and I went to hold her, feed her, and bond with her daily. The day that I got to bring her home from the hospital was comparable to winning the lotto. Then, I remember so vividly, waking up early on the morning of February 15, 2007, for my sweet baby's morning feeding. But what I discovered was like a scene from a mother's worst nightmare. I was distraught at the sight of my lifeless baby girl. She was so cold and blue, and there was blood staining her tiny face. As I thrust her chest, I begged for her to "BREATHE FOR MOMMY," but she couldn't! Why won't she breathe??? This was the question my heart was screaming silently, so loud! As I administered two rescue breaths, my heart raced because I would have given her my last breath if it meant she could breathe again. But she did not, and she never will again. The devastating reality that my baby would never breathe again took my breath away. For the second time in my life, I had no desire to live. I suffered severe depression for months, but I had responsibilities. I had no other choice but to Get Up! So, I put on my familiar mask, went back to work, and school and life, and continued in my journey of mediocracy. The small voices in my head never stopped reminding me that I was the cause of my baby's demise. If I had never considered aborting her, she may still be here. Over the years, I encountered countless, pointless relationships that led me back to my worthless shell and contributed to my walking trauma story. Tired of my sad story, I decided to become celibate and rededicate my life to Christ. In doing so, I felt a sense of relief. Then, one day, I ran into a guy who was respectful, and kind, and so different from the guys in my past. He loved me and my children, and I was finally, truly "happy." No masks, no forced laughter, just love and pure joy. This guy appeared to be everything that I had prayed for, and more. When he got on one knee and asked for my hand, I just knew he was heaven sent. Or so I thought! We did not have a perfect relationship, but what relationship is? The day I said "I Do" was one of the happiest days of my life! After being married for several years, and weathering relational storms, I still loved him as much as the first day I fell. Just a month shy of our fifth wedding anniversary he decided that he was not happy and wanted to separate. You could not even imagine the dagger this was to my heart. It BROKE me!!! I was so broken that I lost all sense of hope in men, and women for that matter. I found my mask, reapplied it, and continued to live in my story of trauma. I tried to drown out the disappointment by throwing myself into my work and school full force, but the voices in my head never stopped reminding me that I was not good enough. Would I ever be good enough? In the next 21 days, you will see how I found the answer, and how it changed my life!

# Day 1

One dark, cold night, I laid awake thinking about the misery that kept meeting me. The pain I met at every turn was unbearable. I heard loud, harsh voices, saying "You're too broken," "You're too damaged," "You're too insecure…" As I sat there unconsciously enjoying my pity party, drenched in tears, sobbing, and feeling sorry for myself… A still, sweet voice began to whisper in my ear. I can remember this voice so vividly destroying every negative image that had been drawn in my head. With each "But," "Why," "Woe is Me," came a direct, dominant distraction to all the crutches I had built. So, this conversation went on for a moment, but its content will envelop my heart for the remainder of my days! The voice simply whispered, "You are…" "You have been…" and "You Will Be…" See, the voice was combating every negative connotation that life's experiences had built in my head. From that moment on, I was inspired to drown out the negative voices in my head and cling to my freedom!

**Today, You Are Free!**

Think about your life and some thoughts or beliefs that may have held you in bondage. What are the things you are being set free from?

_____

_____

_____

_____

_____

_____

_____

_____

_____

_____

## Day 2

Have you ever looked in the mirror, and despised the image that you were viewing? This was Me! I tried so hard to see something beautiful, but much to my disdain, I found myself, broken, damaged, and disgusted at who I had become. It was not until I decided that enough was enough, that I began to take a deeper look. I was able to look beyond the wounds, betrayals, and heartache, and find the sweet and gentle girl deep within. I had a long conversation with her and told her that she was always enough!

**Today, You are Enough!**

Take a good look in the mirror of your heart and take a moment to write about the things that you see.

_____

# Broken Image

Staring at the mirror all flustered,

because I couldn't recognize the image I was viewing.

Unfortunately, however distorted the view, it represented all

that I was and all that I'd ever seen in me.

A spirit as broken as the fragments of glass seeping through the

reflectors...

A discontent heart wishing to find something more in that

image, but I couldn't...

After countless dramatically life altering experiences,

and ill treatment by those in whom I placed great trust.

What image did I truly expect to behold? Me?

See, I was viewing my existence through dirty distorted lenses.

Lenses so tarnished by negative connotations of others, and

wounds often self-inflicted...Conflicted!

In a battle between what I see, and everything I ever dreamed I

could be...

Piecing together broken fragments of a broken image was

tough.

Leaving my hands bruised and my heart more broken, I feared

I'd never be enough...

Until one day I decided to discard all the old pieces and

completely begin again!

Replacing all the broken pieces in sight with Love and Light...

and affirming daily that I'd be alright... that even with my

fragments, I've always been enough...

And I always will be!

# The Mirror Experience

After months of attempting to untangle from my previous married life, I partnered with a church where it felt like my pastor got all up in my business every Sunday and inspired me to seek Christ on a different level. Beyond partnering with the church, I joined the clean team and began to serve in the House of God. Most importantly, I started paying my tithes faithfully. I was then, introduced to a small group called Arise Wounded Women. In this group I was able to unpack my life's trauma in a safe place (besides in my dreams). I acquired several tools that would help me establish boundaries for my emotional safety and find an unconditional love for me. In one particular group session I was encouraged to identify the lies that the enemy used in attempts to destroy my future. These lies were defined as the limbic mirror held by satan. On this invisible mirror, I identified my irrational sense of independence. I have always held the attitude that I do not need anyone for anything. If I allowed myself to depend on someone, I was setting myself up for disappointment. I also identified my strong feelings of inferiority. It had been engrained in my heart that I was never good enough for anyone, so I worked double time to overcompensate for my "worthlessness." I believe the greatest lie within was that everyone's intent was to hurt me. I remember so vividly asking my estranged husband why he hated me so much, and why he got so much pleasure out of seeing me damaged. This belief is partially why I maintained emotional distance between myself and others for most of my life. But the reality is difficult because we all have an innate desire for human connection. How do you authentically connect with other humans when it is so hard to trust them? This is a question that stained my brain for so long, and with strong conviction, I created many counterfeit connections. I would give only parts of myself restricting the innermost elements of me. I offered the "pretty" parts of me. The parts that would be perceived amiable and acceptable in society. I never wanted anyone to see what I saw every day when I looked in the mirror. The insecurities, the fears, the disappointments, the deep-rooted pain, and desires to shatter that mirror. I made finite decisions about my life based on temporary situations. After reflecting on my limbic mirror, I realized that I had been viewing my life through the lens of my trauma. I was blown away by the statement, "you become what you rehearse". I had rehearsed so many negative connotations about me for so long that they had become integral elements of my identity. I told myself that I was too flawed to matter, until I became too flawed to matter in my own reality. As encouraged by my group leader, I began to search the Bible and find scriptures that signified hope, love, and purpose. The text that I initially applied to my life was from Romans 12:2, it read "And be not conformed to this world; but be ye transformed by the renewing of your mind..." From that moment, I committed to a total transformation. If you know anything about transformation, you know that a dramatic change takes place. Once I allowed my mind to begin its renewing process, I began feeling better about myself. My victim mentality came to a halt, and I started my journey to my victory. I was getting so strong! Stronger than before, but not nearly as strong as I could be. I began to value myself more every day. I even said things like "I am beautiful, I am loved, no weapon formed against me shall prosper." And for once in my life, I began to truly feel like I was enough!

# <u>Day 3</u>

For so many years, I wondered why I was never good enough for anyone. Then BOOM! I realized that I was never going to be good enough for another, if I wasn't good enough for me. See, it was never them, it was always me… It was me who devalued me and accepted less than I deserved. It was me who measured my worth by their standards, without having any of my own… Oh, but I'm better now! And hunnie, can't nobody tell me I'm not beautifully drippin' in melanin, with pretty eyes and nice, thick thighs, an unforgettable smile, with intellect and self-respect, who's sensual, responsible, loving, kind, oh and love for the grind!

**Today, You are Unique!**

Take a moment to think about how you will authentically show up in the world today.

_____

_____

_____

_____

_____

_____

_____

_____

_____

## <u>Day 4</u>

As a young girl, my mom would tell me a story about a man who traveled a long way daily. Though the story never mentioned where he was going, it is to be assumed it was somewhere of importance. Now, on his journey, he found himself on the ground. He had slipped and fallen in a hole in the road. You would think that the man would choose a different route the next day, but he kept going the same way and he kept falling in the same hole. I don't know about you, but I was just like the man in the story. I kept taking the same route and getting the same results. But the beauty in each new day is the opportunity to begin again. The definition of insanity is doing the same thing while expecting different results! If we want to change our circumstances, we must change our direction.

**Today, You are Mindful!**

Thinking back on some experiences that you've encountered! As a result, what are some things you will do differently in the future?

_____

_____

_____

_____

_____

_____

_____

_____

# <u>Day 5</u>

A few years ago, I was headed to the bank. Not intentionally in a hurry. But in an attempt to get around a slower moving vehicle, I switched lanes. As soon as I got over, I was hit smack dab in my tail end. While waiting for the authorities, I thought to myself "Dang, I should have stayed in my lane!" You see, both lanes would have gotten me to my destination… but, needless to say, I never made it to the bank that day. I tried to operate in a lane that was not meant for me. We all have specific gifts, talents, and roads we are destined to travel. When we operate in a lane that is not for us, we run the risk of causing collisions. These collisions may add to the negative images already drawn in our minds. Choose to be exactly who you are, with no apologies!

**Today, You are Predestined!**

Take a moment to think about your life, and all the experiences that made you who you are. Have you discovered "Your" lane? How would you describe your lane?

_____

_____

_____

_____

_____

_____

_____

_____

_____

## <u>Day 6</u>

One day, out of boredom, I decided to do some research on birds. While I learned a lot of interesting facts about a plethora of our fowl friends, I was most fascinated by the Eagle. Many see eagles as a symbol of beauty, bravery, courage, focus, and grace. With all the powerful qualities of the eagle, its strongest is sight. Their eyes are specifically designed for long distance focus with clarity. I have heard that "Where there is no vision, the people perish" (Prov. 29:18). Before you can get to where you are going, you have to know where you are going!

**Today, You are Focused!**

Think about the dreams and goals that you would like to accomplish. What are some steps that you can take to move towards them?

_____

_____

_____

_____

_____

_____

_____

_____

_____

_____

## **Day 7**

One day I was drinking tea and my baby asked for a drink. Before I even thought about it twice, I had given her the remainder of my drink. Just a few minutes later I realized that I was still thirsty, but my glass was now empty. It was then that I remembered that I could not pour from an empty glass. The revelation is that I am useless to my purpose if I am not being filled consistently. I would like to pose a rhetorical question…

How are you refilling your glass? As a parent, it is so easy for me to get wrapped up in everyone else's needs with no attention to my own. I learned a long time ago, that you have to make sure you are good before you can take care of everyone else.

**Today, You are Overflowing!**

Think of all the ways that you have been there for your loved ones and made everyone else satisfied. Now, how will you commit to refilling your own glass?

_____

_____

_____

_____

_____

_____

_____

_____

_____

## Day 8

Have you ever been stuck? Just stuck! Not in a physical place, but in such a negative head space. I know this scenario all too well, as I have been there a time or two. At one point I was so stuck that it affected my parenting, my productivity, my performance at work, and even my physical health. Sometimes we can be so broken, that we can't even imagine ourselves whole again! We know that satan comes but to kill, steal and destroy. I want to let you know that he cannot have anything else that belongs to you... He CANNOT kill your Hope, steal your Joy, or destroy your Destiny! Period! You are more than a conqueror and no weapon that is formed against you shall prosper. God is about to "Re-Member" you in the eyes of those who tried so hard to break you!

**Today, You are a Conqueror!**

Think of a time that you felt stuck. What did that place teach you about who you were?

_____

_____

_____

_____

_____

_____

_____

_____

_____

# <u>Remember Me</u>

Lord Remember me, please remember me, but not just remember me..

RE-MEMBER me!

See, the broken pieces that you see, they didn't get here cautiously,

I was reckless with my heart, somehow that broke us apart..

that dude was supposed to love me, but he hurt me instead,

and all the dirty things he did be staining my head...

I lost my dignity, my confidence, oh yea, and my respect.

I used to be a good girl, but I must confess now I'm such a mess...

I used to love my neighbors and treat everybody right, but now these broken pieces gotten wantin a fight...

So now I come before you, knees to the floor, crying out to you cuz I can't take no more...

The lies, the tears, broken promises, and fear...

God, only your power can pull me outta here....

So, when I say remember me, I mean re-member me...

I mean re-member all the broken parts that no one else can see...

Just like humpty dumpty, put me together again...

re-member the parts of me that can't love anymore...

I just need you to heal, set free, and restore..

remember the pretty girl that I used to adore...

The one who loved music, and laughing and fun..

I wanna be close to you, I don't wanna run...

Please, RE-MEMBER me!"

# Day 9

One sunny, summer day, I remember playing in the pool with my children. Although I can't swim, I was enjoying my time in the water. Playing a game called Marco Polo, I slipped under the water and panicked. For a second, I thought I was drowning. After a few seconds of "drowning" and losing my breath, I heard a small voice say, "just stand up." See, I stood taller than the water and there was no way that I could actually drown if I just stood up. Though the pressure made it difficult to stand, I did... And then I could breathe again! As you journey through life, I hope you will remember that you are bigger and stronger than whatever you may face. All you have to do is stand!

**Today, You are Strong!**

Think of a time when you thought it was over but realized that you were just not standing in the right position. In what areas in your life do you just need to "stand up"?

_____

_____

_____

_____

_____

_____

_____

_____

_____

_____

## <u>Day 10</u>

Out walking, and I saw a young man walking with his toddler baby girl. He was holding her hand and she seemed so carefree. It was as if she knew that she was protected. As they reached the curb, he said "watch ya step babygirl." She struggled to get her little feet down, so he picked her up and carried her the rest of the way. As I reveled in the beauty of the moment I was viewing, I was reminded of a time when my father, God, carried me through a severely painful season. I need to let you know that you do not have to walk alone. He will hold your hand to guide you and carry you when you struggle to carry yourself!

**Today, You are Protected!**

Think about all the ways you have worried yourself over tricky situations. What are some areas you need to be carried through?

_____

_____

_____

_____

_____

_____

_____

_____

_____

_____

# **Day 11**

Working with a trainer at the gym, he advised me to add more weight. Confused, I asked why, but I adhered to his instruction, nonetheless. He explained that as the workout gets more vigorous, my muscles will get stronger. Initially, it wasn't too bad, but... then my thighs began to burn. When I felt like I couldn't go any further, he said "you wanna see results, don't you?" The extra weight was uncomfortable, but my progress was remarkable. I had to press past the pain for my gains. If we are not continuously pressing ourselves, we will never get the results we desire!

**Today, You are Persistent!**

Think of a time when continuing was too painful, but you couldn't give up. How will you exhibit persistence in your life?

_____

_____

_____

_____

_____

_____

_____

_____

_____

## Day 12

In a hurry to get to work, I could not find my keys. I looked all over the house and tore up my room. After a few moments of frustration, I found them in my pocket, where I had placed them earlier. I hindered the arrival to my destination by looking in all the wrong places for what I needed. I had to learn to stop looking all over for what I needed because it was already in my possession. You do not need validation from anyone to be who you were destined to be. You are absolutely amazing, just the way you are. This is your invitation to be unapologetically you!

**Today, You are Equipped!**

Think about who you have been, who you are, and who you aspire to be. If you could be anything in the world, why would you choose to be you?

_____

_____

_____

_____

_____

_____

_____

_____

_____

_____

# <u>See Me</u>

The most painful state of mind is when you realize that the

only person you want to love,

doesn't only want to love to you...

What's even more painful is that you still desperately long for

this love, and offer it, knowing it may never truly be returned,

But you try to live and be and do,

And use the lessons that you've learned...

Time and time and time again, only to get burned...

 Again...

You've spent your life trying to save the world, but no one sees

that you need saving too,

You feel like someone should see the pain in your eyes,

and the constant lies, like...

I'm fine and I'll be alright...

No one can see your heart ripping in three, while

you're screaming inside...

 Somebody See me!

 See the me that loves so passionately, the me that will give

my all just so someone else doesn't fall...

The me that loves music and purple and dreams,

The me that finds solace in supporting other people's streams...

Is anyone there, are they watching me sink?

But no one is there, and no one can see...

So, you stop and think, and think and think...

and just when you're on the brink, of a massive

breakthrough...

You begin to truly see... YOU!

# Day 13

Nothing impacts your self-image as strongly as matters of the heart. When you trust someone with your heart and they break it, it often damages who you believe you are. I have had my share of broken hearts and the misery it brings, and it is soul shattering. I remember so vividly, lying prostrate on my bedroom floor, crying because I felt so invisible. After many disappointments, I found myself alone again, left to deal with the messes that someone else had made. It was in that exact moment that I discovered the value of self-love. See I had neglected to offer myself the love that I was expecting from everyone else. If you don't grasp anything else that I say, please know that the love that you give to yourself is more valuable than any love that you'll ever receive.

**Today, You are Loved!**

Think about the love that you give to others, and how you show up for yourself. What are some ways that you will commit to loving yourself more purely?

_____

_____

_____

_____

_____

_____

_____

_____

_____

_____

_____

## Day 14

I was looking at a drawing of an elephant one day... Initially, I saw an elephant with five legs. Intrigued at the evident inaccuracy, I began to look at the drawing from different angles. It was then that I realized that it didn't have five legs at all. At times, life can be like an optical illusion, we perceive specific elements, and our minds tend to fill in the gaps. This may also be known as the concept of perspective. The truth is, your circumstances may not change, but if you change your perspective, it may change your life. It's time we start looking at life from a different angle, perhaps the more positive one!

**Today, You are Insightful!**

Think of a time when things were just bad. How could you have changed your internal outcome by changing your perspective?

_____

_____

_____

_____

_____

_____

_____

_____

_____

## <u>Day 15</u>

I love to write! I have been writing since I can remember.
There is something so calm and relaxing about writing,
whether it be creative writing, journaling, or poetry. The
incredible thing about writing your own story is that you get to
revise the parts that don't suit you. While realistically you may
not be able to alter your story, you can always shift the
narrative. A narrative is defined as the message received
through the story… And you get to create, translate, and
demonstrate your own narrative!

**Today, You are Creative!**

Think of a time where you could have shifted the narrative to
suit your satisfaction. How would you re-create your story?

# Me Too

Saw her friends supporting her,

I whispered Me, too?

Saw the way he loved her,

 And I whispered, Me too?

I was at the park one day,

and hoped someone would look my way.

Instead, they looked the other way.

So, I whispered Me too?

She got a promotion,

 And she got a new whip,

Everybody's flexin,

I ain't even got a coin to flip, but I whispered,

Me too?

Decided to try something new,

Thought they would all cheer for me, but the looks on

their faces screamed "booo"

All that I can do was sigh,

And… I whispered, Me too.

When will it be my turn to be noticed and feel

loved?

Sadly, I may never know.

Oh, but when it comes hurt and pain,

Man, all I feel is Me too!

# Day 16

As I was driving one day, I watched a man allow his dog to poop on his neighbor's lawn. It must have been the most disgusting thing that I had seen all day. It prompted me to ponder on all the times that I had allowed people to poop on my own lawn. Not in a literal sense, but every time I gave voice to those who did not mean well, who tried to tarnish my name, who distorted my self-image... Sometimes the greatest gift you can give your future is distance from negative influences. It is tough to release what has become comfortable, but it is so necessary! No closure, no animosity, no reasoning, no reconciliation... Just deuces!

**Today, You are Courageous!**

Think about your life and all the experiences you have had. What influences should you be removing from your life?

_____

_____

_____

_____

_____

_____

_____

_____

_____

## **Day 17**

Feed an ant, you will attract more ants. Feed a seed, you will bloom a flower. Feed your imperfections, you will produce insecurities. Feed your fears, you will develop anxiety. But if you feed your faith, you will grow stronger. I learned a long time ago, that whatever you feed will grow. It will be at your best interest to start feeding those things that give life and starving those things that distract you from your purpose! Use wisdom to determine what requires nourishment and what you should be starving.

**Today, You are Wise!**

Think of people and things that have been distracting you from your purpose. What are some things that you may need to stop feeding?

_____

_____

_____

_____

_____

# Finding My Pretty

One of my greatest challenges has been accepting who I am, as I am. I always felt like the ugly duckling in my family, in temporary friend circles, at school, and at work. I have overheard family complimenting others on their beauty, but it felt like it was never me. In my young adult life, I even heard an old boyfriend on a phone call saying, "she's not the prettiest but I love her." He never knew I heard the statement, but it has haunted me through many relationships. In the back of my mind, I would always wonder if men were really attracted to me. I also wondered whether I was too big or too little, if my face was too fat, whether I was too dark, or my butt was too big. I began to define my beauty by my scars and often attempted to cover them up. I could not grasp why people could never see the beauty in me, all the while it was me who couldn't see it. Well, I did have some males who told me I was beautiful, but a close friend (at the time) once told me that they only looked at me because I had a big butt. I know it sounds crazy, but I received that message and, many others that were similar and applied them to my life unconsciously. One day, not too long ago, I was having a phone conversation and I muttered, "I may be ugly, but I'm not stupid." My daughter, who was about 13 years old at the time got really upset. She said "Mama, you're not ugly." You see, she looks just like me, so if I think I'm ugly then I must feel the same about her. Just the opposite is true though; I think her dark melanin blend manifests an untouchable beauty. I learned a very valuable lesson on that day; I had to be very careful of the words that I was speaking. I desperately needed to find my pretty, so that I could give it to my daughters when they needed it. At first, it was like a game of *Where's Waldo*, searching for an image in all the wrong places. To find my pretty, it was necessary to destroy all the images of beauty plastered in my mind from negative words, the media's superficial definition of beauty, and comparison to others. I committed to rehearsing my affirmations and speaking kindly to and about myself every day. A drastic changed took place, when I made a conscious decision to get rid of the old, distorted mirror and look at my life through the mirror defined by my purpose. This is when I became Pretty By Design! I now knew that God had made me uniquely equipped for the destiny he planned for me, way before I could even see the Me that I was born to Be!

# Day 18

After taking my first Teacher's certification exam, I was excited to receive the results because I had studied for numerous long nights. Much to my disappointment, I had missed the passing score by three points. This was excruciating for me, as I took great pride in my intelligence. Needless to say, I did not feel so smart at that moment. We all encounter situations that do not go as planned, and failure stings... May I submit that failure is just a seed for future your success? You do not Go through inconvenient situations; you Grow through them by using the lessons they teach you.

**Today, You are Growing!**

Think about some situations that you have encountered. What lessons did they teach you, and how can use them to fuel your future?

_____

_____

_____

_____

_____

_____

_____

_____

_____

_____

_____

## **Day 19**

During childbirth, women are encouraged to take slow, deep breaths through contractions (pain). This helps the mother-to-be to focus and it sends necessary oxygen to the seed that she is carrying. As she breathes, it brings about a calmness to her, and distracts her from the pain she is feeling. Sometimes, life just hurts! Like a woman in labor, we need to make a habit of breathing through adversity and focusing on the seed that we are carrying. Perhaps, our resolutions will be found in our focal point. Don't let adversity stifle your gifts, because the world needs them!

**Today, You are Gifted!**

Think about the gifts and talents that you hold within. How will you commit to protecting your gifts? How could you be using your gifts to impact society?

_____

_____

_____

# Nothin' Sweet

Ain't nothin sweet about revenge,

See, what's sweeter is the damage that bliss does to the

emotional spirit beater,

You ain't got time to combat

what she said, and he said, or they did,

So, pick yo chin up,

And stick yo chest out,

Chile, you hold infinite power,

And you rule your world,

Everything you think you need,

You already got,

Don't worry about those fools,

Cuz yo spot is yo spot,

You know, mama always said,

Somebody gone always have something petty to say,

You strut yo magic,

And flip yo hair,

Bald or wigged,

Locced or faded,

Short hair, don't care,

Sprinkle that pretty dust everywhere,

You don't owe nobody nothin,

Not even acrimony,

Come on now,

It's a death ceremony,

A tragic demise to the trauma sent to cease the gifts that lie

dormant within,

To the antagonistic images of what she said, and he said, or they did,

To the voices in yo head,

Sayin you're too small or too big,

Too dark or too bright,

If you wanna see clearly,

You gotta walk in the light,

In the light you'll find that every opposition was merely a figment of vain imagination,

And you ain't got time for no reconciliation,

No need to conform to society's lies,

You walk by,

They chatter,

You look back and smise,

You know, Smile with ya eyes,

You have no competition, no comparison, no equal, And after you baby,

Ain't gone be no sequel,

We gone bury what she said, and he said, or they did,

Cuz baby,

Ain't nothin sweet about revenge!

# Day 20

One night while out driving, I had to turn my head briefly because the headlights on a passerby's car was so bright! But that did not stop them from passing or shining. Light is made of energy, and the energy that you exude is illuminating and valuable! Sometimes people are threatened by your light, and some will do just about anything to discourage your glow. To be quite honest, you should never dim your light for anyone. Someone somewhere is waiting to see it!

**Today, You are Radiant!**

Think about the shape that the world is in today. Who can you share your light with?

_____

_____

_____

_____

_____

_____

_____

_____

# Day 21

Sometime ago, I was walking down the road and stumbled across a huge dog. Naturally, afraid of the attack, I dropped everything and ran. Now, my dilemma was that I dropped EVERYTHING! Someone once told me that it is more dangerous to show fear in the face of a dog, because it actually incites the attack. When facing life's turbulence, it is even more dangerous to drop the things you need, like your peace, your joy, your love, or your character. I need to encourage you today… At the point of attack, run if you must, but don't drop your things!

**Today, You are Victorious!**

Think about the things that you may have dropped on your journey. What are some of the things that you are committed to holding on to?

_____

_____

_____

_____

_____

_____

# A Moment to Breathe

When life gets rough, as it sometimes will, I often refer to a technique called "deep breathing." Breathing reduces tension and helps you to relax; and it sends oxygen to the brain which increases brain functions. Breathing has many other benefits, but the most vital for me is the strengthened ability to focus on what really matters. I hope you will try some deep breathing in the future. As you inhale, usher in thoughts of things that make you happy. As you exhale, envision yourself releasing any negative energy. Here is an acronym that you may rehearse as you practice your breathing:

**B**e present, and fully in the moment.

**R**emember, it's only a season.

**E**mbrace the lesson at hand,

**A**nd apply it to your life.

**T**hink on the solution more than the problem.

**H**old on to your promise.

**E**verything is working for your good.

# <u>Daily Affirmations</u>

I am a gift to the earth!

I am incredibly valuable to society!

I deserve love in abundance, and I will accept nothing less!

I am stronger than any storm that may come my way!

If I can see it, I can do it!

I have vision and purpose within me!

Everything that I touch will be multiplied!

I was created to conquer because I am more than a conqueror!

No weapon formed against me shall prosper!

I am blessed to be a blessing!

I am working to become the best version of me!

I have no competition or comparison!

No one can do Me as well as I can!

I choose to live happy because I can!

I am fearfully and wonderfully made!

I am a beautiful depiction of grace!

I am beautiful, inside, and out!

From this day forward, I will be Authentically Me!

# Your Story

Take some time and produce some affirmations that speak to your story and recite them every day, until they become your reality!

_____

_____

_____

_____

_____

_____

_____

_____

_____

_____

_____

# My Prayer for You

I pray that my words will be a light to you and anyone who has struggled with self-love, self-worth, or self-respect. I pray that God will grant you the innermost desires of your heart. I pray that the plan that the enemy has to destroy anything attached to you will come to an instant halt. Because we know that no weapon formed against you shall prosper. I pray that love and joy will overtake you, and peace will be your portion! In Jesus name, Amen!

# Many Thanks

I am so grateful for my mother, Paulette Rolle, who has always been my greatest supporter. I am grateful for my children, who are my true meaning of love and the reasons why I so desperately needed to change. I would like to thank each and every one who has ever prayed for me, held my hand, wiped my tears, let me slob on your shoulder for support, or just listened to me at my weakest, darkest of hours. Most importantly, thank you for taking the time to read my words or invest in my story. I hope you are inspired, encouraged, and blessed by the words of my heart! And that when you look in the mirror, you see a beautiful depiction of Grace!

Made in the USA
Columbia, SC
15 April 2022